Penelope: The Story of the Half-Scalped Woman

University of Central Florida Contemporary Poetry Series

PENELOPE

University Press of Florida

Gainesville Tallahassee Tampa Boca Raton

Pensacola Orlando Miami Jacksonville

The Story of the Half-Scalped Woman

A Narrative Poem by Penelope Scambly Schott

04   03   02   01   00   99   c   6   5   4   3   2   1

04   03   02   01   00   99   p   6   5   4   3   2   1

Library of Congress Cataloging-in-Publication Data

Schott, Penelope Scambly.
Penelope: the story of the half-scalped woman:
a narrative poem / by Penelope Scambly Schott.
p.cm. — (University of Central Florida contemporary poetry series)
Includes bibliographical references.
ISBN 0-8130-1638-x (alk. paper). —
ISBN 0-8130-1639-8 (pbk.: alk. paper)
1. Stout, Penelope, 1622 or 3–1732 or 3—Poetry. 2. New Jersey—
History—Colonial period, ca. 1600–1775—Poetry. 3. Frontier and
pioneer life—New Jersey—Poetry. 4. Indians of North America—New
Jersey—Poetry. 5. Women pioneers—New Jersey—Poetry.
6. Delaware Indians—Poetry. I. Title. II. Series: Contemporary poetry
series (Orlando, Fla.)
PS3569.C5283P46   1999
811'.54—dc21   98-45484

The University Press of Florida is the scholarly publishing agency for the
State University System of Florida, comprising Florida A & M University,
Florida Atlantic University, Florida International University, Florida State
University, University of Central Florida, University of Florida,
University of North Florida, University of South Florida, and University
of West Florida.

University Press of Florida
15 Northwest 15th Street
Gainesville, FL 32611–2079
http://nersp.nerdc.ufl.edu/~upf

Acknowledgments

A special thanks to the Lannan Foundation for a Senior Fellowship at the Fine Arts Work Center in Provincetown, Massachusetts, which provided time and space to write this story.

Thanks to the Hopewell Museum and to the Hopewell Public Library in Hopewell, New Jersey, where Beth Miko and Barbara Orr helped locate research materials.

Thanks also to the New Jersey Council on the Arts/Department of State, for a 1998 Fellowship in Poetry and for their previous support as well.

Preface

This narrative borrows from historical and literary sources. Where little is known, much is invented. No offense is meant to Penelope Stout's numerous descendants, many of whom populate our local phone book.

Penelope lived in New Jersey in the seventeenth century. This period saw sporadic warfare between the native Lenapes and the growing numbers of Dutch and then English colonists.

Penelope's second husband, John Richard Stout, was one of twelve patent holders of eastern New Jersey, and two of their sons were the earliest white settlers of Hopewell and the Amwell Valley.

A Grandson Remembers Penelope

Johnny, put your hand
in the pocket of my garment
and feel the scars of my wound;

that you will know that it is true
and you can tell your grandchildren that it is true, and they
  can tell their grandchildren that it is true

    And Johnny did
    and it was all true.

Penelope Kent Was Born

In Sheffield, England, 1620.
My mother died of my birth.

Father was banned from his church.
But Holland is a gentle land

where even Jews may live,
though Father prefer not.

I read Latin and Greek
poorly. But early on

I met Penelope of Ithaka
and would not wish to wait

so long. Now I am twenty
and strong and tall:

it all
unravels.

Penelope Keeps Clean

I rub the soot
from the candle snuffer;
I sift dead ashes
from the tiled stove.

We do not have servants,
says Father. *We are servants*
to the Lord. I am servant
to Father.

Father sends me to the baker
(he will not go himself);
Father sends me to the bleeker
to fetch home strong bleach.

We are clean in the sight
of the Lord.

       I am clean
in the mirror. I am clean
in the caves of the body,

a clean, unbroken vessel.

Penelope Sees the Rabbits

Early one morning
I take up my basket;
     the women are washing
     the cobbled streets.

I go to the butcher
where the slit rabbits
     are wearing their cufflets
     of gray fur.

Who can imagine
to be such a rabbit?

And behind the rabbits
on the inner wall,
     hangs a small painting:
     a woman with peaches,

a woman with light
caressing her face;
     and I want to be
     that same woman

lit by that same
unnameable light.

     The painting? I ask.

The butcher massages
his double chin:

     Leyster, says he,
     one Judith Leyster,

     a dame, but she knows
     how to wiggle her brush.

Penelope Meets the Painter

I seek her out that same afternoon—
Father in his study, the rabbit on its spit,

spotless linens on the taut line.
She asks me in and bids me sit

and lays on my skin buttons and lace
as at home I do not wear. In a chair

like a painted throne she limns me forth,
candles flaming in plain day. They say

that painting is Devil's Work:
her three apprentices—imps at her call.

Light from the window in leaded squares
falls on my shoulder: a Spanish mantilla.

If lace is the web of the Devil, I am wrapped
in infernal coils, my cheeks ablaze,

her gaze as a lover might gaze, I think—
I have no lover—brushing each limb

with orange fire. *The butcher will pay*,
says Judith. *He aspires.*

Judith, my Ley star, my pole star, my Circe
and sister flesh. You wake inside me

all the mirror hides.

I cannot tell my father
I am become a graven image,

and shall return.

Iconographies

Our old stories
destroy us

unless
we tell them new.

This Penelope
doesn't need me,

but I need her.
We are sisters

here, groping
for air.

Making images
is dangerous,

but so is not.
And repetition

makes a braided rope
of scraped sinew

knotting my hair
back from tears.

Penelope Kent's Marriage of Convenience

New Amsterdam,
they call it,
across the sea.

Father calls it
Opportunity.

It would be
unmaidenly

to go alone.
My groom is known

to Father.
He would rather

a true believer,
but he believes

in old family:
van Princis.

Once

I meet the young man.
He has pale, unmarked hands.

His father
will pay for my father

to publish his treatise
on Divine Justice.

What justice in marriage?
His kiss tastes of porridge.

Judith, Goodbye

Call me Penelope van Princis.
Call me not. We are leaving.

The ship is in port,
our trunk in the hold,

my maiden linens
starched and folded.

Judith, goodbye.
I drop my face

to her plump bosom
and weep and weep

for my dead mother,
my harsh father,

the vain husband
I barely know.

It is not he who showed me to myself.

Judith's Picture

Judith points to her easel: *Vastanavond.*
The Night Before Lent. The Last Drop.

Where two young men carouse, the one
in brown, the other a pink satin dandy,

van Princis, I think, disloyal, and see
him smoke and drink, the other tipping

a gourd-shaped jug. And behind them both,
invisible, the skeleton
with sinking hourglass and skull.

      We should not step upon that deck.

Misbegotten Voyage

We slept aboard
the anchored ship,

its furled sails
my wedding veil

I want sons,
said my husband

and thrust on home,
and then we did not sail.

Further cargo,
said the captain

many golden guilders
in the heavy metal coffers
of New Amsterdam Company

I went back to my father's house
and polished candlesticks;

six weeks later
we set to sea.

I will not speak of the long storm,
    the waves like castles rising up,

        dashing our faces, my blanched husband
        clinging to his bed.

My breasts tingled and grew tender;
   I was willing to love him.

   Cool cloths I brought him,
      and bouillons and custard blanc,
        all that the ship could muster.

He walked on the deck, holding my arm.
My breasts throbbed, and my skin was warm.

Aground at Sandy Hook

She's breaking up, yells the boatswain.
We wake and stagger to the rail.

Long breakers roar toward the beach;
the moon is early but small.

    Our Father who art . . .

        . . . and now in the hour of my death

I lead my tremblous husband down the ladder
and drag him through surf.

    Where is the harbor,
    where are the docks,
    where the waiting governeur?

Salty and soaked,
our little company considers.

Fire, for God's sake, a fire,
whimpers van Princis, and shudders.

Our leader refuses: *We hear*
the savage Natives in these parts
are fierce inclined for war.

Next morning, they leave,
heading along the shore
for New Amsterdam, sand
and gravel under their feet.

My husband is ill
and cannot travel.

    We will send for you, they promise.
    And vanish.

        My namesake safe in Ithaka,
        and I, Odysseus now,
        cast on this barren coast.

The Savage Natives Here About

They come with fishing nets and weapons,
bow and arrows over the shoulder
and a stone axe tucked at the belt.

Three, tall and well formed,
all young, their heads shaven,
except a feathered center crest.

First they see the broken boat
stuck on the shallow bar, and speak
among themselves, and now see us.

    Swift butchers. First my husband:
        an axe to his back. He groans once
            and falls. The loose and reddening sand.

    Now three upon me. Fast. Each
        to destroy. My belly axed open
            my arm nearly off   my hair yanked back

and half way cut   away from my skull,
    and the sea and the sky turn black
        and black and black and nothing at all.

    Moonrise over the wrecked spar:
    with one arm I gather my glistening
guts and crawl toward a hollow tree,

and I see one star.

Alive in the Tree

My husband asprawl on the sandy ground.
His waistcoat ripped down the back.
He has died as a stranger dies,
the last van Princis, at the edge
of the dark fish sea. Crows circle,
and I am distantly sorry.

But closer, here in the shell of my tree,
a plunge as if again of the boat,
and my stomach all gaping and lurching again;
and one hand that I think might be mine
grapples and clutches and enters the viscous
hollow; tips of my fingers pulling away

all sticky and spotted with dark flecks.
The gray rabbits in Jan Ochtervelt's Butchery,

        how he split them wide open,

and I wonder my own blooded hands
bear no cufflets of fur.

Miscarriage

Father bade me go
Cleave unto thine husband
I do not like that word CLEAVE

It is a meat axe

Go forth and plant, said Father,
the seed of faith in a pagan land

My womb has emptied,
The seed of faith
was not van Princis' seed

And now, for the first time,
I dare to look at my feet
at the white and bloody doll

flaccid across my feet,
still in the silken sack, skin translucent
with veins like rivulets in cheese,

and I name him: *My First Son*

and would gather him up

and tuck him back,
        but the slick ropes of my guts
            barricade my womb.

Hunger

The stab and the burn and I bite on the back of my
   hand
and the taste is of rust, and the salt makes me hungry
   for bread,
and I close my teeth on the bark of the tree,
but a ridge of the bark scours raw
the gouge in my scalp, so I jerk up my head
and it hits on a ledge that protrudes from the bark,
   and I'm banging my head
           sideways and back,
                   as hard as I can,
to knock the soul from my painful flesh,
and my forehead stops on a rubbery ledge,
and I open my eyes
and the sky is as blue as a flat sea.

At the level of my mouth, a giant fungus
blooms from the bark of the tree, and I chew
and I chew, and the milky excrescence
is nectar and brown ale.

After Eight Days

I eat of the mushroom and drink of the dew.
Seven times the moon rose from the ocean
rounder and brighter. An owl flutters:
the soft *shuu-shuu* of its fringed wings.

Sometimes I sleep. Something with claws
took my baby away. The porcelain face,
closed eyelids, curved arch of his brow:
gone. Scraps of sack at my swollen feet.

Numb, and thirst, and dark, and light,
and always the mushroom that grows from the tree,
and the tide on the sands, its pebbled roll,
and a long log that turned over and over

riding in on the surf. It didn't touch him.
Once the water darkened his waistcoat,
but then it withdrew. Eyes in the dark.
At sunrise he sags like a soaked rag.

On that eighth morning they come. Two.
The young one took his bow and poked
at the body, indifferently, and took
from it nothing. The other, older, paused

as if in thought, and made to join
the first who strolled ahead. *Wait*,
I call, *wait*. How must I live
to see the moon grow small again?

And yet it seemed I could not die
unless by grace of savages. *Here*,
I call, *please*, though they know not my tongue,
and yet are made like other men.

The younger swings about, reaching
and lifting his terrible axe
and I rejoice. Too soon. The other
seizes his hand. *Saa*! *Saa*!

      as if to say *For shame*. So thus
      am I discovered. His robe from his back
      he takes, and lays me therein, and swings
      me through the woodland to this place.

Lamentations

I am placed on a shelf
in a long shed.

The air is sweet smoke;
under my cheek, thick fur.

Many faces.

A-kee'! A-kee'! chant the women.
They wear nothing on top.

Indian Medicine

I am an empty cask.
Clean water floods my belly,
the guts set gently back.

With needles of fish hook
and sutures of vine,
they lock up my skin.

A poultice of molten resin
singes the loose seam.

      Someone is screaming.

          Now I am sleeping on board
          and the smooth sea pains me.

Haircut

He shows me a sharp flint.
Why will they kill me now?

It's the man from the beach
who hauled me home on his back.

He crouches and saws at my hair;
it falls away like a dead pelt

matted with stiff blood. *Gold*,
said Judith, of my old self.

Machk, says the man, and points
to his greased chest.

What the Women Know

I keep on bleeding
from the dark crease.

The old one, Hu´ma,
her fingers like a spider,

gives me no peace.
She pulls at my arm

where it bends wrong
and drags me along

to the hollow tree.
We scrabble in humus:

there, in leaf-mold,
a piece of the cord

which we bury fast
under a straight ash.

She pats my empty womb:
my sons will be strong.

Penelope Makes Pottery

Who knew the worth
of an iron kettle?

We walk miles
to dig clay,

the whole day
swallowing spittle.

In a grass-lined pit,
balanced on its tip,

a bowl grows
coil by coil;

I use hot stones
to make it boil.

According to Hu´ma
I am a good squaw.

Penelope Meets the Corn Goddess

I pour blue corn
from a clay vessel:

wooden mortar,
stone pestle.

Oh, Hosanna
Ka-hay´sa-na

To pound
is to pray.

After Many Moons

They come from New Amsterdam
with firearms.

A white woman with heathen
is never right, say the Burghers.

Better I died on Sandy Hook beach;
I would cause them no problem.

The charity of Christian folk
is beads, cloth, an iron pan,

and the thunder rod. The god
my father serves is blind.

I stand behind Hu´ma and Machk
but am forced to go back.

The Half-Scalped Woman

Here in Gravesend
children point;

after I pass,
little boys laugh.

I will never again
take off my cap.

Courting

Here's what I like
about John Richard Stout:

> he speaks English
> he owns land
> he has strong hands

Here's what I learn
about Mr. Stout:

> he loved the wrong woman
> so his family sent him to sea
> and now he wants me

I say, Give me a lusty man
I say to John Stout, *Yes*

Penelope's Second Wedding Night

My uncle, Mr. Applegate, keeps open house
for neighbors and me and Mr. John Stout:
aged cider, a hogshead of good beer,
and even, God forgive, a fiddle-man
and all the English here about.

> Father would say
> he hath fallen away
> from Faith.
> In faith
> say I, what harm
> in making cheer?

To rollick and frolic and laugh,
to raise a carafe to the bride—

and had I died, I would not come
to him, my strong and eager groom.

Behind the heavy curtains of the bed
the winsome barnyard romp,
the bump and pant and gasp
and lying back, and then he asks:

> *You didn't bleed*, says John.

> He backs away and lifts the candle
> to my damp face. Something dark
> in his eyes. *That Indian*, he says.
> *Did he, did you? With one of them?*
> and cannot speak.

Now I sit up, hands on my hips,

and stare him down. *Mr. Stout,*
I am a widow.

Tonight I am full with his seed.
He tosses his head with the pride
of a great bull. We will breed
a tribe.

Wedding Present

News moves fast on forest trails,
words float by canoe.

They know I am married.

Up the shore, across the harbor
this stranger has carried

a skin bag of bear grease.
He lays it on the threshold.

I send to Hu´ma
a pewter tumbler.

We Move Across West River to Middletown

I speak to John of good land,
wide reaches and straight trees
and all the shellfish at the beach.

Too many neighbors make hard labor;
they take small quarrels to court.
Game grows scarce, patience short;

John puts the plantation for sale.
He wants to start again
across the river, among my friends.

As ever, he asks about Machk.
I recite my week in the tree,
how gently he carried me back.

>   We travel by boat and cart,
>   bring yoke and leather.

>   We travel together
>   and feel well married.

Big Belly

John is tender with me now.
I show him how, with my big belly.
I say, *There are ways,*

funny man.
We find many ways.

Salvage

The soul is flotsam
of sea foam and dust.

Twirl your stick
in its socket of dry wood:

fire

pierces
the old wound.

The shell of the world
cracks loose.

Who so fierce
as a woman in labor?

Only
the gaping, hollow sea.

Penelope pulls for shore.

I Know to Be Careful

Full-term and bawling,
but I know to be careful:

babies are loosely attached
to this earth.

I dress John Junior
in my husband's old shirt

to fool the ghosts.

Thin strips of corn husk
I tie to his wrists.

Squaws come to the garden
with tiny shoes,

holes cut in the bottoms.
Hu´ma instructs him:

> *When the ghosts come,*
> *oh, little one,*
> *you will say:*
>
> *See*
> *I have holes in my shoes*
> *and cannot travel.*

Penelope Bears Her Third Living Son

When I rise from childbed,
Machk stands at the back door,
silent. He never comes in.

He brings me *w-tee'heem*;
we call them strawberries.
Wa-ni'shee, I say. *Thank you.*

Mother Penelope, he calls me
gravely, the only English words
he knows. I show him the baby

and he goes.

Misunderstanding Leads to the Pig War

Me-sing´ in the skin
of a bear

rattles the shell
of a turtle.

This pig was eating
my corn;

now I am eating
this pig.

How can you own
an animal?

An animal owns
itself.

Wealth is one's own
work:

go down to the ocean
and cut wampum.

The Warning

He enters the winter kitchen and squats
beside the lighted stove and waits.

—*Machk, are you well? Is there sickness
in your village? Tell me that sickness.*

—*A-kee,´ alas.*

He tells it: his people no longer want
our houses, fences, cattle all over
their hunting grounds. Will burn us down.

—*Go to the tupelo down by the creek.
    Do not sleep in this house. Go.
      Look in the reeds. Take my canoe
        and your babies and row.*

John doubts but helps me load the boat
and shoves us out from concealing reeds.

—*May you come to no harm.*

—*Nor you, my own.*

He will wait with his gun by the barn.

The Deal

Here my husband tells his tale:

>*—They came with whoop and weapon*
>*out of the woods. As the roar*
>*of the lion who leaps on his prey.*

And John took out his clay pipe.
and lit it up, and spoke
in English, Dutch, and Delaware,

all mixed: *Smoke with me, friends.*

>*Just yesterday we traded buttons,*
>*you and I, for venison and beans.*

And gave tobacco all around.

>*Let us confer by light of day,*
>*and I shall make you good amends*
>*and I shall pay.*

>This compact
and alliance we intend to keep.

Tonight I sleep at home in peace.

Gam'wing Festival

September, and Machk comes again.
They have counciled, the wise ones,
and decided: I am invited. Not John.

I strap the babe to his cradle board
and travel through the forest.
The central post of the Big House

is the staff of the Great Spirit
rising to the twelfth heaven:
twelve heavens, twelve days, twelve masks.

Me-sing,´ the Solid Living Face,
guardian of all the beasts,
is carved onto a living tree

and then removed and painted:
red on the right, black on the left
for all things opposite, east and west,

day and night, best and worst.
I too am all things double, my head
half blond, half bare. The bonds

of longing and choice stretch
through my hair, right and wrong,
woman and man, chorus and song.

The silence
of one owl is louder
than the clatter of turkeys.

Ceremonies of Safety

The tree is the story,
and each story is holy
to someone.

Three centuries later
another Penelope
chose this story

and am not sorry.

      I crawled into the tree
      of my own small children
      and hoped I was safe,

      but I let men fire
      the base of my tree
      and the bark smoldered,

      so I cut off my hair
      close to the skull.
      Now I am older

and care

less. The base
of Odysseus's bed
was a living tree;

the base of my tree
is Penelope, blessed
by survival, this veil

of borrowed tales
across her cheek.

The Meadow Plays Its Ah-pee'kawn
for Three Penelopes

Come.

You are not woman or man
    or child. You are wind.

Rake your airy fingers
        thus,   through reed grass.

Let burrs ride your shoes.
    Blow cottonseed away.

Open the bramble gate
    into the pale green sky.

Come in, trills the meadow.

    Each life is a noise
        on the planet, smaller

    than the palest tendrils
        creeping up fence posts

    here in the meadow
        where you serenade

    the little shadow
        of your name.

Penelope Stout Names Her Daughters

Mary, Alice and *Sarah*:
for my mother, and John's,
and Abraham's old wife.

I wonder, after twenty years
was Penelope too old,
Telemachus an only child?

> I never thought I'd live
> to have so many children;
>
> now I will live forever.

The Family Thrives

Today is washday.

I go to the crabapple
and it spreads me a table.

I go to the willow
and it sheds me a pillow.

I go to the paper birch
and crouch in its white arch

below the copper beech
which is old and rich

in its smooth ironwood bark.

But yesterday

I went past the box elders
where the woods are wilder

and out to the field juniper
which is even further;

up through the fields I went
where I was meant to be,

on up to the great oak,
and the oak spoke,

and it said to me, *Now*,
it said, *now and always*,

grow, so I do.

Raising Many Children

John is away
trading cattle.

I settle here
on this hard bench

to rest for a moment,
hands in my lap.

Mama, Mama.
Their busy voices.

I finger through linsey
the glossy branching

of the ivory scar
across my womb

as I hum:

>   *from here, from here,*
>   *there sprouted forth*
>
>   *each living soul*
>   *within this room.*

Machk Draws Me a Story

We are out in the summer kitchen.
He plucks a coal from the cool fire.

> *This is a tortoise lying in water:*
> *circle with paws and head and tail.*

> *When water runs off his high back,*
> *a single tree grows from the shell.*

> *It sends forth a sprout and a root*
> *and a second shoot.* He draws in dirt:

First Woman and First Man. *And from*
these two were all produced.

Still

as a tree, he hunkers back on thin
haunches and lets me serve him lunch.

He eats with the spoon on his belt.
I have felt the scales of the turtle

under my feet.

Moccasins

Len-hok-si'na, they call them,

which my Dutch and English neighbors
refuse to pronounce.

I cast off my heavy shoes
and step lightly.

Do I shame my pretty girls
in church?

Blessed by Good Men

I live in the shelter
of two strong trees. These
   are my roof posts raised high,
   my beautiful old men.

Deep in my secret mind
I imagine seeing them swim,
   touching the girth of their limbs under water:
   hairy and smooth, pale and bronze.

Loving them both with my eyes.
Loving my own long strength.

John Richard Stout's Last Will and Testament

I give and devise unto my loving wife
during her natural life . . .

> Natural, John? Each day
> a miracle; I, your good right hand,
> with my left arm crippled.

. . . all my orchards, house and cellar,
and all the land I now improve . . .

> A solid man; and he worked hard.

I give and bequeath unto my loving wife,
all my horsekind, excepting one mare and colt

to my son Benjamin—son of our old loins—
for wintering my cattle.

> And now our older boys say I should leave
> this house and come into their *sauer landt*,
>> deep woods as yet uncut,
>> and winter camp of my old friend.
>
> When Machk-the-Bear comes to invite,
>> I gladly saddle up and ride.

The House with the Fence

I sit in the house in the forest
at the edge of the Indian track
that runs from river to river,
Raritang to Delaware,

and go nowhere.

Ne-hu´ma: I am Granny.
My son Richard has built a fence
to fence the cousins in. When I add,
I have thirty-eight living grandbabes.

Hu´ma they call me, like the old woman
who washed out my wounds. I am older
than she. They do not live so long
as ours, but better I think. Deeper.

Perhaps I have lived too long
in houses: plaster and floral papers
in parlors; sometimes I miss
the fresh scent of rushes.

I Move Out and In

I move out of my body and into my mind,
but my wounds remind me.

Nobody told me growing old
was so needy.

Widow woman, widow woman, widow woman.

I think often of Judith and my young skin:
None of my children suspects

I am the same
maiden within;

I ought to warn my daughters.
All these years I thought

my eight days in the tree
had stripped me clean

of want. Now Judith
comes to me at night.

John, John,
I am haunted

by wanton dreams.

Penelope's Grandchildren

—What are you doing, Hu´ma?

   —Counting the trees.

—But the trees are too many to count.

   —Then I am counting the leaves.

Penelope and the Painter

Look! Somebody comes.
Not preacher or peddler.
A white man with a brown pack.

     —Mornin', ma'am. Fine spell o' weather.

     —Out with it, man: what do you want?

     —Only to paint your picture.

Sixty years to the month, and I sit now
for this country limner as I sat once
for the prize student of Frans Hals.

Where Judith gave me laces and silk
and a pewter bowl, the limner paints
me with nothing at all. Only myself,

a plain old woman; what I contain
has come forth from me, and no one
can change my condition. The man

has no skill, or less, but I bless
his ambition.

Penelope's Great-Grandchildren

—What are you doing, Hu´ma?

    —Listening.

—But everything is quiet.

    —That is Kook´hos-the-Owl
    flying

    out of Neshanic mountain
    to the place of two creeks.

    Someone is dying.
    I think it is Machk.

    Hoo, hoo, I too
    soon will fly with him.

Asleep Beneath the Buttonwood Tree

—Hu'ma, it is raining. Come in.

    —Yes, child.

        It takes the turtle

        a long time to get somewhere

        but it knows where it has been.

Mother Penelope Is Buried
in Middletown in Glory

Three daughters and seven sons;
by the time of her death in 1712,

five-hundred-and-two blood descendants
and just one story;

if she had been Odysseus instead,
to sail the whole known world?

But listen: the spirits of four winds
twirl and bend to this one place.

In the tree it began; in a stone, it ends.

He Who Creates Us by His Thoughts

The World and everything in it
>is made by Him. These are his helpers:

the Sun and the Moon and Keeper
>of Corn, and *Me-sing´* who rides

on the back of a large deer
>keeping the animals well.

He also creates the words and the songs
>and puts them inside of our heads.

On the day Penelope took off her cap
>and the side of her skull was bare

she pushed back her long, white hair
>and lay down on the pillows

of the great, high bed, and withdrew
>into the hollow tree of her soul,

and the sons who found her there
>knelt. This was long ago.
>Long ago.

>>*Wu-la´mo. Wu-la´mo.*
>>My story is woven.

Glossary

ah-pee´kawn	little flute
a-kee´	alas
Gam´wing	twelve-day Big House ceremony to thank the Great Spirit
hu´ma	grandmother
ka-hay´sa-na	Mother Corn
kook´hos	owl
len-hok-si´na	moccasins
Machk	Bear, a name
Me-sing´	mask, guardian
ne-hu´ma	I am Granny
saa	shame
sauer landt	Dutch, for *red land*, due to the red clay soil; now called the Sourlands
wa-nee´shih	thanks
w-tee´heem	strawberries
wu-la´mo	long ago

The Lenape vocabulary used in the poems is mostly from M. R. Harrington; additional words were taken from the *Walam Olum* and other sources. Accent marks indicate stressed syllables.

Which Parts Are True?

This narrative corresponds with all the generally accepted facts, which are these:

In 1639 the Dutch West India Company relinquished its monopoly whereby only stockholders got rich, and more colonists were attracted to New Amsterdam.

The date of Penelope's birth and shipwreck are uncertain. Her father is believed to have been a dissenting minister who was expelled and forced to move to Holland. Penelope's first husband was named either van Princis or van Principis, and is reported to have been so seasick on the voyage that after the boat ran aground (most probably at Sandy Hook, in modern-day New Jersey), he could not continue the journey on foot.

All accounts place Penelope in a hollow tree. The nature of her wounds is fairly well documented, as are the basics of Indian medicine.

It is unclear how long she remained with the Indians before being returned to an uncle, Mr. Applegate, in Gravesend. Certainly she was among them long enough for her wounds to heal, though she carried the scars to her grave. The words she spoke to her grandson when showing him her wounds came through family tradition into the history books.

Penelope's second husband, Mr. Stout (his first name is given as both John and Richard), owned land plot no. 12 in Gravesend, Long Island, now part of Brooklyn. He and Penelope married in 1644.

These were their children:

John, 1645–1724	Peter, 1654–1703
Richard, 1646–1717	Sarah, 1656–?
James, 1648–?	Johnathan, 1660–1722
Mary, 1650–?	Benjamin, 1667–1734
Alice, 1652–?	David, 1669–1732

Penelope is widely reported to have maintained a friendship with the Indian who rescued her. The name Machk comes from accounts of a local chief who first invited the Stout boys to the Hopewell area. The story of Penelope's rescuer later warning her about an upcoming attack goes back to the earliest sources.

The various outbreaks of violence between settlers and Indians have been named for the causes of the disputes. Thus occurred the Pig War (actually on Staten Island), the Whiskey War, the Beaver War, and even the Peach War.

On November 8, 1665, Penelope's second husband was recorded as one of the twelve holders of the Monmouth Patent. In 1675 he deeded 60 acres each to James, Peter, Mary, Sarah, and Alice. The quoted parts of his will come from local records.

Penelope died in 1712 and is said to have left 502 descendants. In 1715, in the Baptist Church at Hopewell, New Jersey, 8 of 15 members were Stouts.

In 1664 New Amsterdam became New York, and as the English colonists were more numerous than the Dutch, it marked a sad turning point for the Lenape Indians (also known as the Delaware). By the end of the seventeenth century, most of them had died or left New Jersey. Today the descendants of the Lenape live in Oklahoma or Canada, but their language is no longer spoken.

The painter Judith Leyster (1609–1660) studied with Caravaggists in Utrecht and in 1629 moved back to Haarlem. She specialized in night scenes with visible sources of light. She signed her work with "jls" and a star, after her family's Pole Star Brewery.

Her painting *Vastenavond* was completed in 1639 and is now in the John G. Johnson Collection of the Philadelphia Art Museum, where it is called *The Gay Cavalier*. While seventeenth-century Dutch genre painting was widely commissioned and owned by the middle classes, there is no evidence that she and Penelope ever met.

The anonymous itinerant painter mentioned later is typical of early American folk art, but again, there is no evidence that Penelope ever sat for such a portrait.

Sources

Beck, Henry Charlton. *The Jersey Midlands*. New Brunswick, N.J.: Rutgers University Press, 1939, 1962.

Cohen, David Steven. *The Folklore and Folklife of New Jersey*. New Brunswick, N.J.: Rutgers University Press, 1983.

Harrington, M. R. *The Indians of New Jersey: Dickon among the Lenapes*. 1938. New Brunswick, N.J.: Rutgers University Press, 1963.

Heckewelder, Reverend John. *An Account of the History, Manners and Customs of the Indian Nations Who Once Inhabited Pennsylvania and the Neighboring States* 1818. Philadelphia: Historical Society of Pennsylvania, 1876.

Kraft, Herbert C. *The Lenape or Delaware Indians*. South Orange, N.J.: Seton Hall University Museum, 1996.

Kraft, Herbert C., and John T. Draft. *The Indians of Lenapehoking*. South Orange, N.J.: Seton Hall University Museum, 1985.

Ladies at the Crossroads: Eighteenth Century Women of New Jersey. Morristown: New Jersey Division of the American Association of University Women, 1978.

Oestreicher, David M. "Unraveling the Walam Olum." *Journal of Natural History* 105, no. 10 (1996): 14–21.

Pevtzow, Lisa. "Ghost Stories Put a Scare into History: Spirited Tales Unearthed in Sourlands." *Princeton Packet*, July 22, 1997.

The Red Record: The Wallum Olum. Translated and annotated by David McCutchen. Garden City Park, N.Y.: Avery Publishing Group, 1993.

Salerno, Joe. "To Indian John, the Last Lenape Indian to Leave West Essex, New Jersey, in the Year 1761." *Journal of New Jersey Poets* 30 (1997): 2–3.

Smith, Samuel. *The History of the Colony of Nova-Caesaria, or New-Jersey: Containing, An Account of Its First Settlement, Progressive Improvements, The Original and Present Constitution, and Other Events, to the Year 1721*. Burlington, N.J., 1765.

Stockton, Frank R. *Stories of New Jersey*. 1896. New Brunswick, N.J.: Rutgers University Press, 1961.

Stout, J.D. *Stout and Allied Families*. Privately published, Chariton, Iowa, 1991.

Sultzman, Lee. "Delaware History." Lenni Lenape Historical Society and Museum of Native American Culture website, pp. 1–27, 1997.

Walam Olum: The Migration Legend of the Lenni Lenape or Delaware Indians. Indianapolis: Indiana Historical Society, 1953.

Watkins, Jane Iandola, ed. *Masters of Seventeenth-Century Dutch Genre Painting*. Philadelphia: Philadelphia Museum of Art, Philadelphia, 1984.

Weslager, C. A. *The Delaware Indians: A History*. New Brunswick, N.J.: Rutgers University Press, 1972.